SCOTTISH VERSES

Edited By Kelly Scannell

First published in Great Britain in 2018 by:

 Young**Writers**

Young Writers
Remus House
Coltsfoot Drive
Peterborough
PE2 9BF
Telephone: 01733 890066
Website: www.youngwriters.co.uk

FOREWORD

Young Writers was created in 1991 with the express purpose of promoting and encouraging creative writing. Each competition we create is tailored to the relevant age group, hopefully giving each child the inspiration and incentive to create their own piece of writing, whether it's a poem or a short story. We truly believe that seeing it in print gives pupils a sense of achievement and pride in their work and themselves.

Our latest competition, Monster Poetry, focuses on uncovering the different techniques used in poetry and encouraging pupils to explore new ways to write a poem. Using a mix of imagination, expression and poetic styles, this anthology is an impressive snapshot of the inventive, original and skilful writing of young people today. These poems showcase the creativity and talent of these budding new writers as they learn the skills of writing, and we hope you are as entertained by them as we are.

CONTENTS

Aidan Lonnie (8)   70
Oli Gray (8)   71
Jenson Key (7)   72
Megan Simpson (7)   73

Currie Primary School, Currie

Fia Rijsdijk (8)   74
Benjamin Shields (9)   76
Cole Falconer (9)   78
Emily Houstin (9)   79
Amelia Hill-Cousins (9)   80
Fergus Brown (8)   81
Amy Logan (9)   82
Vaila Bruce (9)   83
Colette Inglis (8)   84
Layla Ayton (8)   85
Olivia Gibb (8)   86
Ryan Lumsdaine (9)   87
Brodie Shields (9)   88
Maria MacLean (8)   89
Yanis McLean (9)   90
Erin Kempton (8)   91
Matthew Watt (9)   92
Sophie Williamson (8)   93
Fraser Gordon Simpson (9)   94
Connor Mackay (8)   95

Eastern Primary School, Broughty Ferry

Karolina Nissen & Sahrah Bhatti   96
Cameron Irvine & Rhys Wilson   97
Alyssa Kelly   98
Jude Presley Harper (10)   99
Niamh McArtney (10) & Niamh McColgan (10)   100
Lohgan Ramsay (10) & Summer Julia Hope   101
Harvey Colwell & Callum Gillogly   102

Fair Isle Primary School, Kirkcaldy

Kamaljit Kaur (11)   103

Garnetbank Primary School, Glasgow

Shaheer Tabassum (9)   104

Glencoats Primary School, Paisley

Amez Abdulla (10)   105
Leah Turley (10)   106
Faizan Mehmood (8)   107
Abdlmonem Homam Sharif (10)   108
Dylan Trainer (9)   109
Chloe McCready (8)   110
Charlie Wilson (8)   111
Ellie McGarrigle (8)   112
Casey Lynn Judge (7)   113
Jack Thorley (8)   114
Arran Porteous (8)   115
Lucie Woods (7)   116
Liam Roy (8)   117

Portsoy Primary School, Portsoy

Summer Goodwin (9)   118
Alex Greenwood (10)   119
Ruby Rose Wilson (8)   120
Sandy Abberley (9)   121
Kayla Cameron (10)   122
Jasmine Craig (9)   123
Madison Taylor (9)   124
Maxi Duncan (9)   125
Sienna Bruce (9)   126
Grace Philips (9)   127
Abi Ferguson (9)   128
Brendan Dawson (10)   129
Sienna Louise Angus (8)   130
Callum Faid (9)   131
Fia Ord (9)   132
Teagan Rose McLeod (9)   133
Eden McGrath (9)   134
Shannon Leigh Mutch (9)   135

Lyla Rose Booth (8)	136	Abbi Gordon (11)	168
Olly McKenzie (8)	137	Isla McArthur (10)	169
Bella Mathieson (8)	138	Katie Ellis Blair (10)	170
Cameron Eddy (10)	139	Olivia Giuliana Vanni (10)	171
R-Jay Robertson (9)	140	Jenny McMillan (10)	172
Kyle Reise (9)	141	Eva Wright (10)	173
Riley Ethan McLeod (9)	142	Sam William Tennant (10)	174
Lexi Thomson (9)	143	Caitlin Neil (11)	175
Laura Sophie McManus (8)	144	Janey MacLellan (10)	176
Cian Spratt (8)	145	James King (11)	177
Mason Taylor (9)	146	Isaac Green (10)	178
		Ryan Duncan (10)	179
		Taylor McKay (10)	180
		Ryan Craig (10)	181

St Aloysius Primary School, Chapelhall

Kerys McGuigan (9)	147
Ava Grace Caullay (10)	148
Ciara Smith (9)	149
Holly Panton (9)	150

St Serf's Primary School, Tullibody

Pagan Luna Rose Bernard (10)	151

The Community School Of Auchterarder, Auchterarder

Dylan Williams (10)	152
Kate Tomczyk (10)	153
Brooke Lily Nassif (11)	154
Guy Morton (11)	155
Holly Husband (10)	156

Thorn Primary School, Johnstone

Logan Falconer (10)	157
Elizabeth Jane Ellerker (11)	158
Rebecca Catherine Henderson (10)	160
Cara Craig (10)	162
Damien Elliott (10)	163
Sophie Henderson (10)	164
Nola Belle Salmon (10)	166
Katie Ferns (11)	167

THE POEMS

Shaper And Me

I was on a vacation for a small occasion
To explore the streets of London and have my
adventures broaden
Then I saw a monster eat a small venomous fly
It was a fluff sticking out of a shop
With her feet walking all through the street
Suddenly, it was sitting on top of me!
She said her name was Shaper and that she liked
strawberry flavour
Shaper liked adventures but was terrified of slugs
She asked if I could be her friend
I thought, *what a funny monster who eats bugs
and is scared of slugs*
I taught her to be friendly with slugs
And she taught me how to eat bugs
We became closer and explored London together.

Maya Karthik (7)
Corstorphine Primary School, Edinburgh

Hamster

The Hamster has a fluffy body
She likes to look cute
I meet her in the garden
What a marvellous sight
I ride on her back
She rides on mine
I meet her in the morning
Behind her favourite tree
But Hamster's always last
She sniffs through the bushes
She sniffs through the trees
I start to look for her
But she cannot be found
That's because she jumps out
And frightens me
I try to get her back
But it cannot be done
Hamster giggles like a baby
And she finds it very fun
Hamster does some funny tricks
Then runs off in the sun.

Abbie Grieve (7)

Corstorphine Primary School, Edinburgh

Thunder Paws

I was walking through the forest
In early, early August
I was hunting down Big Foot
When I met a man in a suit.
He said, "Leave Big Foot alone
And go back to your home!"
He sang a poem
An eerie, eerie poem
It went a bit like this
"He's got daggers in his jaws
And giant thunder paws
He'll bite you, fight you, smite you
Beat you, eat you raw
He'll smack you with a thunder paw
'Cause that's his made-up law."

Rory Cutler (8)
Corstorphine Primary School, Edinburgh

My Monster

His teeth are as sharp as ginormous knives
He has red-hot lava lasers in his mouth
He has more eyes than people in the world
His best friend is Mr Somerville because
He taught him how to play football
Oh so good at seeing, not so good at feeding
Hair so green, favourite food bean
He is the baddest in bad history
His claws are as sharp as daggers
Come, come have some fun
His howl is as loud as a pack of wolves
His second favourite food is boiled eye curry.

Jude Thompson (7)
Corstorphine Primary School, Edinburgh

Sparkly's Life

I was strolling along the street
Until I saw some small, scrapy footprints
I followed the footprints
And then I saw some big, dark blue hints
I looked up
It was Sparkly
She was the sparkliest, fluffiest and cutest
monster ever
She goes in every city and hurries
She takes pictures too
I miss her forever
My friends are scared
For me, it was okay
When she comes, she's still my friend
Together we are strong
Like a little bond.

Chelsie Chim (8)

Corstorphine Primary School, Edinburgh

Death

I am a bloodthirsty savage
And I can shape-shift.
I come from hell
The hottest place ever.
My name is Death.
I travelled to Earth.
Once, it was fun
But quite annoying now.
So when I landed
On Earth
I started to kill people
But then I got hit in the back.
So I tried to see
What had hit me
But I couldn't see it.
Thwack! Hit me again.
What luck?
Boom! Hit it dead.
Once again, I died.

Noah Doring (7)
Corstorphine Primary School, Edinburgh

Eye Guy's Diary

Eye Guy was born from a big, ugly face!
He was very good and had lots of pace
Eye Guy was clever
Forever and ever
He went to a wood
With no food
Eye Guy found out that at least
There were other monsters who gave him a feast
The monsters would say, "Let's go to the bay."
But Eye Guy said, "No."
The other monsters said, "Why didn't you say so?"
The monsters went home
Leaving Eye Guy alone.

Mia Burnett (7)
Corstorphine Primary School, Edinburgh

The Badlands

My monster lives at the badlands,
And is scarier than a whole bask of crocodiles,
He has terrible, tough teeth,
And swallows you in one gulp,
His name is Ray.

Nobody comes near him,
And every day, someone throws pies,
And nobody believes their eyes,
He is as black as a bat,
And really fat.

He has jagged jaws,
And he's snake-like,
He has five green eyes,
And each day, he eats like 200,000 people.

Rayan Ahmed (7)
Corstorphine Primary School, Edinburgh

Spark

Watch out, here he comes, the spooky one in town
Spark's fur as dark as night
Who knows what he'll do to you this night
His brain is blank, not one little peek
But even so, he is a little cheeky
He's got rotten teeth that bite your bones
And every night and day you'll see him in his clothes
His disguise is great so not one person knows who he is
All he likes are prickly thorns
And stealing people's number bonds.

Ellie Calder (7)
Corstorphine Primary School, Edinburgh

A Weird Friend!

Bob was born in Silly Land
He has a blue belly
He has ginormous jaws
My monster has three chubby legs
He has an orange, red, pink and blue face
He will bite you
He has claws like cat paws
He has horrific hair
His feet are as clean as a dolphin's
He is as bad as a robber
His punch is as hard as John Cena's
His favourite hobby is football
He is as fierce as a tiger
His eyes are as small as tiny stones.

Grant McIntosh (7)
Corstorphine Primary School, Edinburgh

Darkfang

I am as sly as a fox
All who enter my kingdom must die
Even the master all should fear.

My talons are sharp
And I like to shape-shift and trick.

And because I am clever
It makes tricking easy
And does the same to shape-shifting.

The food I hunt for
Is a minotaur with
Giant, snake-like horns
That lives in the sea.

And as my name is Darkfang
It means I am always seen in a blur.

Eve Mei Lee Irving (8)
Corstorphine Primary School, Edinburgh

I Am Joggle

I am spiky
And I look scary
People think I'm bad
But I'm nice and friendly
My spikes are as sharp as knives
And I am a monster
With claws that are
As fluffy as teddy bears
I have a bumpy mouth
I am tall and thin
My hole that I live in
Is as dark as night
And as loud as a washing machine
I look as mean as a dragon
But I am as bright and helpful
As a queen
I am called Joggle.

Anna Paterson (7)
Corstorphine Primary School, Edinburgh

My Friend

I was in my bed with a ted
I woke up like a pup.

I slowly got out of my bed
And fled away and quickly
The thing followed me
It said, "Hi, I'm Pilly.
I have eaten twelve chocolate bars
You do not know what I look like
So I will show you."
She had a purple tongue
And her eyes were yellow
Her face was pink
Her hair was red
And she was full
From all the food.

Lily Clark (7)
Corstorphine Primary School, Edinburgh

Greig

I am as big as Big Ben
I am as gentle as foam
My name is Greig
I know every sum in the world
Nobody can see my head
So I am really upset
I want to be smaller
But I can pick up lots of things
I'm as young as a seven-year-old
I love football with my brother
Because he's giant too
But I'm not allowed in a football club
Because I'm too big
So I'm kinda sad.

Fraser Greig (7)
Corstorphine Primary School, Edinburgh

Cutie

I once saw a monster, she was cute
And she was mute
She was very shy
She liked to hide away all day
She was clever, fluffy and funny
She went around with her tongue out
And that looked very strange
She only had one friend - me!
She had lost her family
She was sometimes a bit sad
And wanted to go home
But she couldn't
Because she didn't know where to go.

Jessica Hendrie (7)
Corstorphine Primary School, Edinburgh

15

The Oni-Killer

The Oni-Killer has the legs of a snake
And four arms like Garmadon
It has armour that is unstoppable
The Oni-Killer has a pirate hook for a hand
All his mouth does is scream
It is slimy, sticky, snake-like
Savage and bloodthirsty
The only thing that his eye does
Is shoot laser beams
And eat people up
He can make a time portal
And go into other dimensions.

Ray Govenlock (7)
Corstorphine Primary School, Edinburgh

Camouflaged Charlotte

I was walking home from school one day
When it jumped in front of me
It was a monster!
I tried to run
But it grabbed hold
"Come with me," it said
She introduced herself as
Camouflaged Charlotte
I said, "Hello."
And told her I was Isla.

She took me to Africa
The sunset was beautiful
But soon I had to go
Home to tea.

Isla Samuel (7)
Corstorphine Primary School, Edinburgh

Ooky Oggy

Ooky Oggy was born
In a pile of custard
He had brown, flabbergasted hair
And loved to eat mustard.

He had fangs as white as paper
And eyes as black as coal
He was friends with something strange
It was a little black mole.

One day, he went out
Of his little custard home
Then started to walk towards the village
All, all alone.

Maha Tanveer Hameed (8)
Corstorphine Primary School, Edinburgh

18

Billy's Busy Day

Once upon a Monday
A monster goes for a walk
Along the riverbanks
The river is as blue as the sky
Billy goes back home
Billy lives in the forest
Under a hill
Billy goes out again
And he makes a friend called Fifi
He went to the beach with Fifi
And went to the restaurant called Monster Munch
Billy went back home
And had a big sleep.

Mia Allan (7)
Corstorphine Primary School, Edinburgh

Monster Poem

I am not to be feared
I hug you when you're bad
And when I am angry, I grow a whopping three
feet
My name is Fluffy
I hide in the woods
My hair is like plastic
And I have a bow in my hair
My bow is as pink as a pig
I have no legs
I am made of hair
My teeth are as yellow as the sun
People think I am scary but I am nice and friendly.

Hazel Sandeman (7)

Corstorphine Primary School, Edinburgh

Terrifying Terror

Once upon a Wednesday
A red-eyed, slithering, naughty monster
Walked around a brown, leafy tree
And was feeling as
Naughty as a dog
Doesn't know, not yet, what he is
Going to plan
Maybe a tale or
Maybe a talk
But we'll never know
And never will
And a message from him
He told me,
"I will always be there."

Lauren McKenna (7)
Corstorphine Primary School, Edinburgh

Big

My name is Big Belly
As big as the universe
And when I went to get my pizza
I got hit by a van
When I got back up
I was as tired as staying up 'til lunchtime
When I fell asleep
This little sly bee came through
My window and stung me!
It hurt like being in a fire.
In the next day, my friend
Disco Dereck came over to play.

Daniel Farrell (7)
Corstorphine Primary School, Edinburgh

Molley Monster

Oh jolly, it's a good day for me
It's so sunny today
I wish you could see
Oh Molley, it's so hot.

I wish you were here
I wish you were here
It's so sunny here
I wish you saw me steer.

Where are we, where are we?
We're somewhere nearby
Are we halfway yet?
I think with a sigh.

Kate Waterston (7)
Corstorphine Primary School, Edinburgh

My Monster

Fluffy Florens
Only comes
Out at night.
She doesn't bite.
But she goes
To school
At night.
She has
Ten friends.
She likes to
Be cool.
She is
Very clever.
She's pretty.
She is good.
And she
Likes her
Food.
She lives
In Orlando.

And she
Likes the
Beach.

Georgina Neillings (8)
Corstorphine Primary School, Edinburgh

Skullcrusher

There once was a monster called Skullcrusher
He was as fierce as a tiger
He was as ugly as a big, fat toad
He was as stupid as a yoghurt
His armour was as shiny as pure gold
His skin was as green as a gecko
His dimension was as cool as an anglerfish
His club was as spiky as a hedgehog
His mansion was as hard as stone.

Finlay Scott (8)
Corstorphine Primary School, Edinburgh

Fluffy Fiona

Fiona, Fiona, Fiona
As furry as can be
Her eyes
Are
As drippy
And as red
As blood
She has green
Slimy
Goo coming
Out of her
Nose.
Big, purple fur coming
Out of her
Enormous, round
Tummy
Like the fluffiest
Candyfloss ever
Watch out!
This is my monster
Fiona.

Aoife Power (7)
Corstorphine Primary School, Edinburgh

Glitter The Unicorn!

My monster's name is Glitter
She is very pretty
She is clever and caring
She likes to eat Fruit Loops
And drink rainbow juice
She is as fluffy as a rabbit
She likes people but she can be a bit shy
She lives in the mountains
With her family and friends
She has a fun life
But it can be tricky sometimes.

Eve Fraser (7)
Corstorphine Primary School, Edinburgh

Helpful Hattie

Helpful Hattie is a smarty
And is lovely, clever and cute.

She is very nice and likes
A slice of chocolate cake.

Cake is her favourite
Thing to eat.

We play all day
In the summer.

And I hide
In the shower.

She doesn't really like it
Because she is dripping wet.

Harriet McCaw (7)
Corstorphine Primary School, Edinburgh

Chaos Keri

Keri loves chaos
She sees your bloody bones
Every night and day
She comes to kill your souls.

So watch out in the morning
She might be waiting there
Ready to kill you
And your souls as well.

So be ready for her coming
Every night and day
Her goal is to exterminate
Everybody in her way.

Jayden Foster (7)
Corstorphine Primary School, Edinburgh

Slime Monster

I am called Toodles,
I am eight feet tall,
I was born in the Land of Slimy,
The Land of Slimy is huge,
I can fly high up in the sky,
I am as slimy as a slug's trail,
I have lots of friends to play with.
I can swim deep down in the sea,
I have been to all different countries,
My enemy is Hate Monster.

Kaisar Khir (8)
Corstorphine Primary School, Edinburgh

Blibyboba

Blibyboba was a hero,
Whose favourite number was zero
He was so good,
He never ate food
If Blibyboba was bad,
He would be very sad
His head looked like the sun,
Which made his life really fun
He owned a pet dragon,
Which carried a giant wagon
His wagon was his car,
Which could travel very far.

Sam Mackenzie (7)
Corstorphine Primary School, Edinburgh

Silly Sara's Poem

Well, I am from the Kelpies
I am really friendly and love the sweetie shop so
much
I am as soft as a bunny rabbit
I am as hairy as a hare
My arms are as wiggly as jelly
I have terrible teeth
I am the kindest monster you have ever met
My eyes are as cute as a baby leopard's
I have amazing rainbow hair.

Rosie Brown (7)
Corstorphine Primary School, Edinburgh

Inky

I once travelled to Mars
And met a monster called Inky
He shot lasers at me
I escaped and set a powerful bomb
He tried to escape!
But he was stuck to it
And then Mars exploded
And he was left alone in space
Then he found dynamite
And swam to Earth
He set the dynamite
In a secret cave.

Tommy Bateman (7)
Corstorphine Primary School, Edinburgh

My Monster

My monster has...
Her hair as cosy and fluffy as dog's hair,
Her horn is as flat as a rubber,
Her name is Blue-Blue,
People think she's naughty but she's not,
Her eyes are as small as green peas,
Her legs are as short as Rubik's cubes,
She comes from the unicorn forest.

Kirstie Mae McLaren (8)
Corstorphine Primary School, Edinburgh

My Pet

Bubblegum is my pet,
A very strange one,
His arms are fishwings,
Which I find weird,
He lives in a magical cloud,
His tongue is as long as a lamp post,
He is as soft as wool,
Which I love to pull,
He could drink a whole pool,
His wings are as rubbery as old bubblegum.

Evie Campbell (8)
Corstorphine Primary School, Edinburgh

Monster Poem

My monster's name is Storm
She has terrible teeth and terrible feet.
She comes out at night and gives me a fright.
She's afraid of white mice.
She hunts lots of bears.
She likes arts and crafts.
She's as loud as a tiger
So if you see her
Under my bed, beware!

Leila Nardone (8)
Corstorphine Primary School, Edinburgh

Ash

Ash is not cute
She is as orange as an orange
And she has three legs.
She has a purple pixie skirt.
She is stinky as a skunk
Her teeth are as yellow as a lemon
She is the queen of all monsters
Her crown is made out of junk
And she hates everything
She is so fluffy!

Pippa Belfall (7)
Corstorphine Primary School, Edinburgh

Monster Poem

I am Henor
I have two horns and eight legs
And three eyes.
I am on a beach
I found a bottle
The bottle was green
It was green because it had some seaweed in it
The seaweed was covered with crabs
One pinched me
It did not hurt that much
Then I went home.

Roch Rodziewicz (7)
Corstorphine Primary School, Edinburgh

Bonnie Bockins

Bonnie Bockins, big and strong,
Bonnie Bockins' terrifying tail,
Bonnie, Bonnie Bockins is coming
He's coming for a nasty night
He's coming for yummy you!
Yummy...
He's a muddy murderer
He has devil, bloody horns
Bonnie Bockins is always there.

Ruby Keany (7)
Corstorphine Primary School, Edinburgh

My Monster

He has giant fangs as sharp as a samurai sword
He is as scary as a radioactive zombie
He has one horrible, yellow eye
His other eye was pulled out in a crazy fight
He has claws as sharp as a ninja star
If you see him
Your hair will turn white
He will come for you!

Abiola Jacob Akinbami (7)

Corstorphine Primary School, Edinburgh

The Lichen Wing

The Lichen Wing lurks
In the wood
If you
Dare to go in, beware
Of the curse!
It is looking for the
Three rubies of vengeance
If you get bitten by it
In three full moons
You will be a Lichen Wing
It wants to rebuild
Civilisation as we know it.

Samuel Harvey (8)
Corstorphine Primary School, Edinburgh

Seadriph's Life

Seadriph lives on a mountain
Below the sparkling sun
The busy town below her
Is bustling like a bun!
Seadriph lives far away
In a land with all your dreams
If you ever meet her
She's as happy as a lark
Whenever Seadriph cries
She lies on her bed.

Charlotte Grant (7)
Corstorphine Primary School, Edinburgh

Master Mine

I have disco fever
Because I was born in
The bin lorry
I have a great
Big moustache
However, the
Hairiest back you
Will ever see
And if you see
I will leave a
Trail of sparkles
Wherever I go
And if you see me
You should run.

Murray Black (7)
Corstorphine Primary School, Edinburgh

Lovely Lilly

Lovely Lilly is clever
But has no friends
Because she has spots all over
And people laugh and think if you get close
You get it too
But she is miniature
So she can fit in my pocket
And I can hide her
From the outside
I'm her only friend.

Rebecca Murray (8)
Corstorphine Primary School, Edinburgh

Monster

It was an ordinary day
When a monster came
Its teeth were as sharp as claws
Its eye was as big as a bottle
Its name was Harry
He destroyed the city
He even destroyed the cars
He broke every house but my one
It's like he knew me and he left.

Melrick D'Souza (7)

Corstorphine Primary School, Edinburgh

Fred

Fred has eyes
As red as
School uniforms
He has a
Body as
Orange as an
Ape.

He's
As bald as
Paper.
He has boosters
As hot as
Fire.

His cannon
Is as red as
Blood.
He is fireproof.

Tom Gibson (7)
Corstorphine Primary School, Edinburgh

The Monster

My name is Waggel,
I am as tall as Arthur's seat,
I eat other monsters,
I have green lean legs
I have a red, yellow, pink and blue body
I have a stick for my body,
I have fangs as long as swords,
Oh so terrifying, that's me.

Isla George (7)
Corstorphine Primary School, Edinburgh

The Terror

The monster was born in Edinburgh
His skin is as green as slime
He has six legs that wriggle
All the time
His eyes are as brown as death
And when people see him
They will run as fast as they can
And they will never come back.

Hamish Booton (7)
Corstorphine Primary School, Edinburgh

Fluffy

I have terrible teeth
As sharp as knives
I sound scary
But I am not
I am as cute as a baby panda
I am the nicest
Monster in the world
I am as fluffy as a teddy bear
I can fly as high as the sky
And I like to read.

Amelia McQue (8)
Corstorphine Primary School, Edinburgh

The Best Monster In The World

Hi, my name is Harry Wallace
I once met the best monster in the world!
His name is Tiny Tim, I love him
He has the fastest, fiery jetpack
He has grey hair
And he has red, rosy skin
He has a miniature mouth
And tiny eyes.

Harry Wallace (7)

Corstorphine Primary School, Edinburgh

My Monster

My monster's name is Cuti Pie.
She's small and skinny and loves to fly.
She's as blue as the ocean.
And she's got yellow spots and tiny dots.
Wherever she goes, her friends go too.
Even if she flies to the moon.

Laila Doherty (8)
Corstorphine Primary School, Edinburgh

Pixsy

I have rainbow hair
My name is Pixsy
And I have wings as big as a whale
I am as clever as a scientist
I live in Glasgow.

She is so cute
I love her!
She is as fluffy as a teddy bear
She is bright pink.

Olivia Somerville (7)
Corstorphine Primary School, Edinburgh

The Jeff

I have four arms
I am as big as a giant
I live in a gigantic lightbulb
My claws are as sharp as knives
I am as clever as a computer
I am so scary
You can run but you can't hide
I am as fierce as Bruce Lee.

Ethan McGuigan (7)
Corstorphine Primary School, Edinburgh

The Fire Monster

Hi, I am Ian
I am the elemental
Master of fire.

My full name is
Incredible Invisible Ian
If I see a water monster
I will kill them.

Arghhh, a water monster!
It's time to battle.

Srinivas Rath (7)
Corstorphine Primary School, Edinburgh

Max The Monster

My monster's name is Max
He is very fluffy
He likes to run and jump
His fur is as blue as the sky
He has sharp claws
He is not scary
He likes to eat fruit
He has two friends, Jeff and Bob.

Zach Buchan (8)
Corstorphine Primary School, Edinburgh

Monster Poem

My monster is very, very good
She is the friendliest monster on Earth
And the cutest as well
She is as friendly as a very kind person
She comes from the ocean
She looks like an octopus but she is not.

Isla Irvine (7)
Corstorphine Primary School, Edinburgh

The Monster Of Yellow Land

He has sharp teeth
And he has claws as sharp as a knife
And he has purple hair
And he is as tall as a skyscraper
As long as a train
As thin as a pencil
People think he is friendly but he is not.

Joe Shaw (7)
Corstorphine Primary School, Edinburgh

Izzy

Izzy
Is as
Furry
As
Candyfloss
She's as
Yellow
As the
Sun
And gooey
She's
As purple as
A plum
She saves
The world
Like a
Super balloon!

Amy Hunter (8)
Corstorphine Primary School, Edinburgh

Bloody Ben

Bloody Ben
Living in a den
He ate blood and his
House did soon flood
He had black wings as
Rusty as metal
He had patches of blood
Dropping on landfill.
He had a green body like goo.

Siddharth Kamath (7)
Corstorphine Primary School, Edinburgh

Bob In The Woods

Once upon a
Saturday,
Bob went into
The woods.

With a horse
That galloped away
Into the woods
Bob has one
Eye as blue as
Water and the other
As green as grass!

Orla Grace Dunsmuir (7)
Corstorphine Primary School, Edinburgh

The Craney

The Craney came from outer space,
And its eyes were like laser beams,
Its sudden stare
Made a dare,
To kill my enemy,
It tried to kill me,
With a stare,
But I reflected it back.

Tom Aitken (8)
Corstorphine Primary School, Edinburgh

The Monster!

The monster walks down the street
He looks around at his feet
He walks down to the beach
And sees someone eating a peach
He runs over and tries to steal it
But touches it and gets a hit!

Finlay Wintour (7)
Corstorphine Primary School, Edinburgh

The Blood Man

The Blood Man used to be a normal man
Until he went in the blood machine
He's got claws and a red axe
He's got a blood body.
Come, grab your flashlight
Listen and work with me.

Dylan Todd Stewart (7)
Corstorphine Primary School, Edinburgh

The Horrible Monster

The horrible monster was born inside a cave
He had no name
He had big, sharp teeth
Purple and orange eyes
Hates my bed!
I am scared to open my wardrobe
I saw him crawl into it.

Freddie Grafton (7)
Corstorphine Primary School, Edinburgh

The Blood Sucker

There is a monster called Googles
He rose from the ground a few years ago
He sucks out blood like a vampire
He is as hairy as a rug
Googles breaks into people's houses at night.

Thomas Struth (7)
Corstorphine Primary School, Edinburgh

Monster Poem

My monster is as fluffy as a furball
My monster is as cute as a hamster
My monster is as funny as jokes
My monster is as small as a rubber
My monster is the best monster ever.

Arlo Elliot McBreen (7)
Corstorphine Primary School, Edinburgh

The Monster's Bad Poem

He has teeth as sharp as knives
And his eyes are as blue as the sea
His claws are as sharp as his teeth
And he is a bad monster
You can run
But you can't hide!

Harris Cooper Stanley (7)
Corstorphine Primary School, Edinburgh

Bierdy's Day Out

There was a man called Bierdy
He had a skunk
And people said he stunk
When he went down the street
People could smell his feet
He liked to eat lots of sweets.

Jamie Laidlaw (7)
Corstorphine Primary School, Edinburgh

The Slime Monster

A monster called Slimey
Lives in Area 51 in the west of America
He is slimy and gooey
He is mean and scary
He will kill you and eat you
So please keep away.

Aidan Lonnie (8)
Corstorphine Primary School, Edinburgh

Lava

Ben Boy
His eyes
Are as
Yellow as
The stars
Ben Boy lives in
A volcano
He's got
Black feet
He is
Black except
His arms.

Oli Gray (8)
Corstorphine Primary School, Edinburgh

Monster Mate

I am a monster bean
With some jeans.

I say, "Gaga waga jaga."
As slippery as a worm.

As ugly as a bug
And as stupid as a jug.

Jenson Key (7)
Corstorphine Primary School, Edinburgh

The Yellow Monster

I am nice
I come out at night
I am as big as a mouse.

My name is Daisy
I like petals
I have five blue eyes.

Megan Simpson (7)
Corstorphine Primary School, Edinburgh

Tiggy The Cute And Kind Monster

Hello, my name is Tiggy,
I come from Candy Land,
I love giving out cookies,
With my candy hand.

I have lilac fur,
I am ever so round,
And with my big, blue eyes,
I sometimes stare at the ground.

I hate seeing people being sad,
It is my biggest fear,
It is truly terrifying,
And makes me start to tear.

I love making people happy,
It's my favourite thing to do,
I also like playing about,
Especially with you!

I love going to Leafy Land,
It's where my parents live,
It's so much fun there,
And I always have presents to give.

Candy Land is excellent,
You always get to share,
Come along one time,
It is terrific there!

Fia Rijsdijk (8)
Currie Primary School, Currie

Big Orange Fuzzball

My name is Furball Dumpling
I live with my friendly mum
She is very friendly
And her fingers are also numb.

I come from planet Nickelback
With my friends, Pom, Scribble and Print
Although they're from different planets
All of us like to sprint.

I like to eat macaroni cheese
With all of my darling friends
We sneak some from the shops
And chomp in street dead ends.

I love all my friends
They always come to stay
We always play football
They come once a day.

I look like a big, orange fuzzball
I've got giant legs that are black

I've got big, green, chubby arms
My eyes are blue like Blu-Tack.

Benjamin Shields (9)
Currie Primary School, Currie

Twirl, Swish And Spin

I am Blimple Print
People in my land are cute but...
I am not!
I love my land but...
I hate people who are cute!
I am colourful but...
I hate colours!
I like to go in a monster car but...
It takes an hour!
My favourite friend is Furball Dumpling but...
I hate your mum!
My favourite food is Monster Hut but...
They do not deliver!
I like to twirl and swish but...
Everyone thinks it's a show.
I love books, I like to read Gangsta Monster but...
It takes five months to read it!
I love unicorns but...
I don't like syrup on them.
I love to play football but...
My friend's honk is too loud!

Cole Falconer (9)

Currie Primary School, Currie

Horror

Hello, my name is Horror
I work at Horresvile Town Hall.
I am 90,000 years old
My favourite dance is the floss
I like to eat everything except bricks
They taste like a number two
I am very lucky to look like a cloud
Because nobody can see me
I can just sneakily stick one of my
Enormous legs and stand on my prey
I hate the other clouds because
They make it rain and everybody runs
Inside to safety from the cold
I can't eat the other clouds
Because they are just air.

Emily Houstin (9)
Currie Primary School, Currie

Laserbeam Godzilla

Laserbeam is deadly,
Laserbeam is smart,
Laserbeam can rip
Anything apart.

His fangs are daggers,
His talons are sharp.
Watch him eat
Your mum's heart.

He comes from the south of Hell,
But don't get zapped by his laser beam eyes,
Or you'll be in for a surprise.
He is only friendly to me.

But he has a story that's going to
Melt your heart.
He got bullied when he was a kid,
But got so angry he turned into this mess.

Amelia Hill-Cousins (9)
Currie Primary School, Currie

Scribble The Scribbly Alien

I'm Scribble the scribbly alien,
In my free time, I scribble like so,
I like to eat pizza and pasta,
I also adore eating dough.

I love to play tennis,
And also football,
With my friends,
I like to boot the ball.

I dislike broccoli,
But love meat,
I love to play music,
And tap to the beat.

I am very scribbly,
And that is what I do,
As I run about,
I slide and say, "Wahoo!"

Fergus Brown (8)
Currie Primary School, Currie

Poper The Clingon Monster

Hello, my name is Poper
I come from far away
I love playing basketball
Because I win every time I play.

I have one hundred suckers
And lots of pluckers
I have twenty-two eyes
I may give you a surprise.

See, when I am thinking
My brain sometimes explodes
I overload it so much
That I turn into a toad.

I am very crazy
Some people may think
When I am very crazy
They might call me a mink!

Amy Logan (9)
Currie Primary School, Currie

Deviler The Jumping Monster

Deviler the Devil Monster
Is always jumping up
Never resting
The only time he said yes was when he said yup.

Always hiding under beds
Waiting 'til the children wake
Always scaring children
When he says, "Do you know the jumpy shake?"

Always in the town
Jumping up and down
The passers-by say
He looks like such a clown.

Vaila Bruce (9)
Currie Primary School, Currie

All About Pippy

My name is Pippy
I come from outer space
My best friend is Zippy
If I didn't have her, it would be a disgrace.

I am very spotty
Well, that's what I think
I have nice blue eyes and crazy hair
I also have three little legs.

My favourite food is chalk
It tastes very good
My favourite drink is KA Juice
It's very fizzy!

Colette Inglis (8)
Currie Primary School, Currie

Monster Poem

I have a monster called Dolly
She is nineteen years old
She is amazing at gymnastics
Her favourite food is fish and pizza
She is really good at maths and writing
Her powers are to freeze people
I am from London and she is good
I would go to the jungle with her
She has rainbow hair and purple skin
She has three legs and two arms
She has red lips.

Layla Ayton (8)
Currie Primary School, Currie

Mavrick The Monster!

My monster's name is Mavrick
He comes from Africa
He loves to eat pizza
He loves to go to Mexico
He loves dolphins too
He is blue and hairy and giant
He is fat and he has horns and one eye
He has fangs and he is friendly too
He has a big brain and long, sharp nails
Mavrick is so much fun.

Olivia Gibb (8)
Currie Primary School, Currie

My Monster Guaczilla

I have a monster
He is called Guaczilla
He is green, big and scary
He has no friends
He is bad
He and I would go to London
We would wreck the city
He likes pizza
He comes from Planet Guacamole
He is 500 metres tall
He weighs 50,000 kilograms
That's my monster.

Ryan Lumsdaine (9)
Currie Primary School, Currie

Flaming Laser Eyes

Flaming Laser Eyes
Is his name
He eats rocks and buildings
Just the same.

He's got spikes and can crush people
That's his game
He's got arrow arms and when someone
Shoots other people
He gets the blame.

Flaming Laser Eyes
Is his name.

Brodie Shields (9)
Currie Primary School, Currie

Katy The Green Monster

She has one eye
She is green
Her favourite food is chocolate
She is amazing at maths
Her feet are a size one.
She has lots of spots on her.
Her powers are to make snow.
She would go with me to Canada
She is called Katy
She is from New York
I love my monster.

Maria MacLean (8)
Currie Primary School, Currie

The Little Dragon

This is my dragon
Toothless, he flies
Very fast, he is as
Black as night.

Toothless has spikes to
Protect him in a fight
He likes where
He lives.

Toothless loves going
Flying to Melody Island
Toothless can train dragons
He got shot down.

Yanis McLean (9)
Currie Primary School, Currie

Zommie Stine, Zommie Life

My monster is called Zommie Stine
He works at Zommie Donald's
He has a favourite dance move
And it's called the Swish Swoss Floss
He comes from Planet Zomm
His friends are Bobby and Horror
His favourite food is bones and veins
Washed down with a glass of blood.

Erin Kempton (8)
Currie Primary School, Currie

Pom Long Legs

My name is Pom
I have such, such long legs
They're fuzzy and orange
They look like clothes pegs.

I have a blue body, also fuzzy
I have purple eyes
I have a big, big smile
I would give you a surprise.

Matthew Watt (9)
Currie Primary School, Currie

Planet Pom Pom

A pink pom pom
Ever so round
With blue eyes
And fluffy legs
With golden eyelashes
And blue horns
With golden wings
And a pink nose
With freckles
Two cute fangs
And a red tongue.

Sophie Williamson (8)
Currie Primary School, Currie

Laser Eye Monster

My monster is called Stink
He is very smelly
He has a big, fat belly
And he eats lots of jelly.

He has laser eyes
And electric fingers
Razor-sharp teeth
And a whipping tongue.

Fraser Gordon Simpson (9)
Currie Primary School, Currie

The Hunter

Harry the Hunter
Is a muncher.

He only eats food
Isn't that good?

Do not beware
He really cares.

He likes to eat cakes
And chocolate flakes.

Connor Mackay (8)
Currie Primary School, Currie

Cathleen The Cloud

Cathleen the Cloud,
Likes to run around,
She is very white,
Which means she's very bright,
And to all a delight.
Her eyes are always closed,
And she doesn't have a nose!

Joey the boy is Cathleen's owner,
Before Cathleen came, he was basically a loner,
Joey is very smart,
And his favourite pudding is strawberry tart!
He always wears a blue shirt
But it always has a bit of dirt.

One day, they found a boat,
Then to an island, they began to float.
They declared the island was theirs,
So they did their prayers.
But soon, Cathleen had to go,
So they both went home.
They said goodbye with a little cry.

Karolina Nissen & Sahrah Bhatti
Eastern Primary School, Broughty Ferry

Jimmy The Cutie Pie

My monster is called Jimmy
Who is also very skinny
He is as blue as the sea
And as tall as a tree
He has three eyes
And loves to eat fries.

One day, Jimmy was hungry and decided to go
Out and find some fries
And when he was walking down the street
He didn't expect who he would meet
And to his surprise, he met the same guy
Who was his best friend at school
And his name was Drew
They chatted to each other
They chatted for a while
They giggled and laughed and smiled for a while.

Now you know that Jimmy could be
One of the coolest monsters in history!

Cameron Irvine & Rhys Wilson
Eastern Primary School, Broughty Ferry

Sticky Worst Enemy

My monster's name is Sticky.
He is so very picky.
He is as tall as a table and he is very playful.
On the first day of school, he tries to be cool and breaks an important rule. Sticky takes monster snakes and stuffs them up his back.

His teacher Mrs Crunch is kind of a grunch.
Mrs Crunch wasn't pleased, so she had a plan up her sleeve.
Sticky came to class as bold as brass.
And when Sticky thought he was alone,
Along came Mrs Crunch who started to moan.

When Sticky got out of school,
He learned an important rule to never trick a teacher at school.

Alyssa Kelly
Eastern Primary School, Broughty Ferry

Meet Gumbo

A month long ago, I met Gumbo.
He was as big as a rock and like a blob, Gumbo
was.

Gumbo had four eyes, a red bow tie, top hat and
moustache
And looked like a rainbow blob.

Gumbo took me to space,
To show me a special place called Planet Rainbow.

We got to Planet Rainbow and all I saw was a
UFO.
Out came an alien who was sticky and green and
looked kind of mean.

As the alien was having a fuss, I told him I needed
a shuttle bus.
Him and Gumbo took me home and they said
goodbye with tears in their eyes.

Jude Presley Harper (10)
Eastern Primary School, Broughty Ferry

Cookie's Adventure

Cookie is mad, as mad as can be.
He jumps up and down and says, "Yippee!"
He's pink all over with yellow here and there
He's five years old with lots of hair.

Cookie's love for cookies is out of control
He eats them all day, out of a bowl.
When he runs out, he does not stop
He just goes and robs a cookie shop.

Cookie suddenly gets lost, lost all alone
When he finds the White House on his own
He has his tea with Donald Trump
But accidentally does a pump!

Niamh McArtney (10) & Niamh McColgan (10)

Eastern Primary School, Broughty Ferry

Fluffball And The Royal Family

Fluffball is a hairy beast, she is very kind
And she has a wonderful mind.
She is very funny, you can even tickle her tummy
She is pink and purple
She is shaped like a circle.

One day, Fluffball went for tea
With the Royal Family
Fluffball got dressed up all nice to go
And have some curry and some rice.

After Fluffball had her tea
She went back home
With lots of glee
"I can't believe I met the Royal Family!"

Lohgan Ramsay (10) & Summer Julia Hope
Eastern Primary School, Broughty Ferry

Mr Fluffy

Mr Fluffy is cute and cuddly,
Although he's shy when he's not bubbly.
He has brown fur and bright blue eyes,
You never know, he could be a dog in disguise.

Me and Mr Fluffy went to the park,
Along the way, we met Uncle Mark.
Mr Fluffy couldn't go down the slide,
All because he was too wide!

When he got home, he was ever so sleepy,
He went straight to bed,
He fell asleep with his favourite ted.

Harvey Colwell & Callum Gillogly
Eastern Primary School, Broughty Ferry

I'm... Right... Here!

I'm the dream you don't want to have
The nightmare driving you mad.
I'm the monster in the bushes in the park
The footsteps stomping in your room
The batty vampire flapping in your bright room
Soon comes darkness, shadow and gloom.
Nasty and horrid, hairy, scary feeling
In the dead of night
I reek and speak while my belly tweaks.
Staircase creaks whilst you sleep
Creeping as your heart is leaping
Singing my werewolf song alongside my friend,
King Kong
Bones rattling and hearing moans and groans
What's that? My fingers down your cold spine
Don't scream... Don't make a sound
I'm right here... Don't turn around!

Kamaljit Kaur (11)

Fair Isle Primary School, Kirkcaldy

Theme

So throw your hands up 'cause it's time to get down,
You'd better make way, I'm the new kid in town!
I float on mist with a great battleaxe,
And I always roll deep with a gang of bats,
So throw your hands up if you're ready to clash,
It's the night signal baby, so party like a bat,
Join me and roll in like a twister,
Better watch out, I'm meaner than my sister.

Shaheer Tabassum (9)
Garnetbank Primary School, Glasgow

I Am Always Here!

A drop of rain is like a sudden knock at the
doorstep
Unexpected, yet often welcomed with a smile
It is Tiny Tiffing, the fluffiest, puffiest, loving,
sweetest monster around
Welcome to stay, let's have a great day with Tiny
Tiffing
Let's go Tiff, la-la-la-la, Tiffing can make happiness
Even if you don't want to laugh
Tiffing is not that tall but it doesn't matter
If you're big or small, fast or so slow
Tiffing is always around to make you laugh
That's me; the cutest, loving, fluffiest monster
around, that's me!

Amez Abdulla (10)
Glencoats Primary School, Paisley

New Friend

I met her in the forest
In a big, deep hole underground
She was all rainbow
And looked fluffy like a pillow
Eyes as sparkly as diamonds
Shoes as pink as pink
I walked over and picked her up
"Who are you?"
She told me her name was Rainbow Ruby
As I guessed, she never really spoke to me
She just stared, I imagined us
In her little home, playing games
And wearing bows and trying on heels
She jumped out of my hand and ran away.

Leah Turley (10)
Glencoats Primary School, Paisley

Undefeatable Monster

My monster is called Slimy Smasher
He is:
As strong as Anthony Joshua boxing
As smart as a uni teacher teaching physics
As slimy as goo dripping down your house
As indestructible as Thanos from Guardians of the Galaxy
As scary as a snake biting your hand off.

I love my monster!

Faizan Mehmood (8)
Glencoats Primary School, Paisley

Mr Caty Is My Besty Friendy!

Mr Caty, floody floody
Mr Caty, scratchy scratch
Mr Caty, always hungry, so I feed him
And we go on adventures together.
He is swimmy, swimmy in the pool
He is angry, angry
He always wants to play with me
When he is sleepy, sleepy
He sleeps on my bed
Me and him are best friends.

Abdlmonem Homam Sharif (10)

Glencoats Primary School, Paisley

My Mechanical Monster

My monster is called Spectre
He is:
As smelly as Mr Twit's armpits
As ginormous as a giant, crushing buildings
As deadly as a fire-breathing dragon
As hairy as Mr Twit's wife
As scary as a charging T-rex.

I love my monster!

Dylan Trainer (9)
Glencoats Primary School, Paisley

My Ugly Monster

My monster is called Stinky Eye
She is:
As smelly as a bin lorry
As ugly as The Grinch's hairy face
As weird as having twenty-one eyes
As crazy as a cheeky monkey
As evil as a vampire.

I love my monster!

Chloe McCready (8)
Glencoats Primary School, Paisley

The Chaos Monster

My monster is called Bunny Warrior
He is:
As strong as Superman
As indestructible as bedrock from Minecraft
As soft as candyfloss
As fit as Rocky Balboa
As stealthy as a sneaky ninja.

I love my monster!

Charlie Wilson (8)
Glencoats Primary School, Paisley

My Monster

My monster is called Genie Long Neck
She is:
As silly as a crazy scientist
As petrifying as Mr Twit's wife
As slimy as a slug
As weird as Minions
As greedy as a hungry pig.

I love my monster!

Ellie McGarrigle (8)
Glencoats Primary School, Paisley

My Monster

My monster is called Bobo
He is:
As cute as a fluffy bunny
As smart as a mad scientist
As helpful as a tired servant
As graceful as Varjak Paw
As fast as a cheetah.

I love my monster!

Casey Lynn Judge (7)
Glencoats Primary School, Paisley

My Monster!

My monster is called Bloody Cat
He is:
As creepy as a creepy teacher
As bloody as a bloody bird
As hairy as feet
As fishy as the sea
As stinky as a very old pizza.

I love my monster!

Jack Thorley (8)
Glencoats Primary School, Paisley

My Monster

My monster is called Strong Deadly Slimy Man
He is:
As ginormous as Godzilla
As deadly as a Titan
As strong as King Kong
As tiny as an ant
As hairy as Big Foot.

I love my monster!

Arran Porteous (8)
Glencoats Primary School, Paisley

My Monster

My monster is called Coco Hates Love
She is:
As hideous as Medusa
As hairy as a grizzly bear
As nasty as a bully
As slimy as a slug
As ugly as a villain.

I love my monster!

Lucie Woods (7)
Glencoats Primary School, Paisley

Rock Devil

My monster is called Rock Devil
He is:
As spiky as a stinger
As evil as a villain
As slow as a sloth.

I love my monster!

Liam Roy (8)
Glencoats Primary School, Paisley

Snufflekins

Snufflekins is a fluffy monster
That lives in outer space.
She lives on Planet Saturn
And has glitter on her face.
She has a friend called Fluffy Love
They live in the exact same place.
Snufflekins is as fluffy as a piece of wool.
Love Island is where they both live
Snufflekins is very kind
She'll do whatever you say!
One day, Snufflekins had a great big sneeze!
She covered up all the wildlife
And she didn't even know how
So I helped her clean it up
And I smiled at her with my friend, Fluffy Love
With the glitter still on my face.

Summer Goodwin (9)
Portsoy Primary School, Portsoy

LMG-64

LMG-64 was from the planet Geo 139
And he knew how to rhyme
He had fur all over his body that glowed
And he liked rivers that flowed.

He arrived on Earth at a bad time
When people were mean, tall and lean
Which he didn't like at all
But after a while, he made some friends
But he realised what he had done
He crashed his spaceship, which wasn't fun
But after some time, he fixed it up
He said bye to all his friends then... *whoop!*
One of his friends knocked him down
And he spent the rest of his life
The wrong way around.

Alex Greenwood (10)
Portsoy Primary School, Portsoy

The Monster Found On Earth

Me and my mum were at the beach,
Then we saw a monster at sea.
So we swam to go and see.
The monster was pink,
She had two wings,
We took her shopping for a dress.
After that, we took her home,
And we did our make-up,
But then she needed to go home.
I asked, "Where's your home?"
Then she said, "It's Blob Planet."
So I said, "Let's fly to it!"
The moon was bright and shiny,
Me and my monster flew away.
We had a disco on Blob Planet,
With all the monsters found on Earth.

Ruby Rose Wilson (8)
Portsoy Primary School, Portsoy

The Meanest Bunny Ever

A bunny and a dragon fell in love
In a molten thundercloud up above
The bunny and the dragon had a baby
But everyone thought it was completely crazy
He grew up into a monster child
But mostly, he was completely wild
He had sharp, killer claws
He also had pointy, dangerous jaws
He went to the fair to win a teddy bear
But the Ferris wheel rolled everywhere
He ran and ran but he got nowhere
It bashed into the helter-skelter
Then he ran into the shelter
The roller coaster came on too
So this led to death, boohoo!

Sandy Abberley (9)
Portsoy Primary School, Portsoy

Fluffly Love

Fluffly Love is as fluffy as a rabbit
And has tiny hearts on her face
She is a kind, fuzzy monster
And lives on beautiful Saturn
Fluffly Love loves rubbers
And I just don't know why.
Fluffly Love has four small eyes
Like little ants on her face
Love Island is where she lives
It is a lovely place
She has little sea-blue eyes
And thick purple fur.
Fluffly Love is the friendliest monster around
She can see the whole world from Saturn
Fluffly Love would love to write
But she doesn't know how.

Kayla Cameron (10)
Portsoy Primary School, Portsoy

The Monster Who Was Too Cute

Cutie Pie the Monster has blue eyes
Cutie Pie the Monster has a brown face
Cutie Pie the Monster has soft and fluffy fur
Cutie Pie the Monster has no friends.

He was lonely and sad with no one to play with
He was walking along the road
He saw someone upset
"Would you like to be my best friend?"
They went to the big, sunny park.

The next day, they went to school
Cutie Pie the Monster was happy
Cutie Pie the Monster had a best friend
Cutie Pie the Monster had a happy end.

Jasmine Craig (9)
Portsoy Primary School, Portsoy

Doughnut

Ring went the bell, the class was in
Doughnut was sad and feeling down
The class was calling her names all around
She sat down in her seat alone and bubbled
Ring went the bell for lunch, everyone was sad
Doughnut was going to steal the doughnut
Then she wanted the doughnut in her belly
She went to the head teacher's office
She was scared
She was frightened and petrified
She got suspended for a year
She never ever stole a doughnut again.

Madison Taylor (9)
Portsoy Primary School, Portsoy

The Bow Cat And The Know Cat, The Monster Cat

The Bow Cat with the Know Cat
The Know Cat was the unfriendly monster cat
He had a friend named the Bow Cat.
The Bow Cat monster said, "Don't do that!
Be the friendly Know Cat."
The Know Cat monster said, "No!
I'm the unfriendly Know Cat."
The Bow Cat said, "Well, if you do that
No one will like you as the Know Cat."
The Know Cat said, "Okay, I will do that."
Then Know Cat was the fun Know Cat monster.

Maxi Duncan (9)
Portsoy Primary School, Portsoy

Fluffy The Monster

Fluffy the Monster came from Pluto
He is happy, cute and fuzzy
He has three cuts on his face from a fight
He is very fluffy and has eight legs
He came to Portsoy one day
He had ice cream with me then we went to Loch
Soy
But he had to go
And when he got back
Something went *boom!*
It was an earthquake
Then it stopped, everything was destroyed
He was so upset until...
Five years went by and it became more beautiful.

Sienna Bruce (9)
Portsoy Primary School, Portsoy

Cutie And Me

Cutie, the most cuddly monster
Likes cuddles but is shy
She comes from Silver Sea
Her friends are Cooly, Twinkle and me
Twinkle and me
Cooly, Twinkle and me
Cutie and me got some ice cream
With the queen in Portsoy
Then we went to the park
We saw Cutie's alien ship
Green, blue, purple and red
Then the queen got a trip back to London
And that left Cutie and me
Cutie and me
That left Cutie and me.

Grace Philips (9)
Portsoy Primary School, Portsoy

Are You My Mother?

Fluff Puff was a monster, cute and fluffy
She had no family, no one
But Twisty was mean and scary
He bullied her until she started to cry
One day, she entered a circus tent
She thought about her mother
The ringmaster of the circus
She found Mother Adeline's cabin
It was a wonderful, whopping cabin
She saw her mother on the stage
Her mother saw her and grinned
And reached out for her hand and smiled.

Abi Ferguson (9)
Portsoy Primary School, Portsoy

Travis

Travis was a happy monster
His hair was long and glittery
He had four legs and six arms
He had big blue eyes
When Travis opened up his eyes
He was in Australia
He looked happily at the sun
He looked at the water
He went inside to get an ice-cold drink
He went outside to go into the pool
He was swimming like a mental maniac
He came out of the swimming pool
And then fell asleep on his chair.

Brendan Dawson (10)

Portsoy Primary School, Portsoy

Monster In The Storm

The monster was walking in the woods
Then he met a furry friend
He was funny and did tricks
He could even juggle with sticks
His furry friend was a water monster
He lived in a long lake
Suddenly, there was a storm
The wind blew them both to the floor
They got up and ran as fast as they could
To the water monster's house
Then they felt better and safe
The friends went back to his family.

Sienna Louise Angus (8)
Portsoy Primary School, Portsoy

Chip

Chip the monster comes from Planet Ketchup
His body is made of chips
His eyes are made of mayonnaise
There's ketchup on his hips
The king sent him on a meteor
For eating the frozen ketchup palace
He landed in the North Sea
All covered in seaweed
He saw a little island with a big sign
It read *Hell Island*
He went there and found friends
And decided to stay on Earth.

Callum Faid (9)
Portsoy Primary School, Portsoy

Snuggles The Glittery Monster

Snuggles is the glittery monster
Lives in a rocket in space
She is a very clever scientist
With golden hair round her face
When Snuggles went to visit Earth
Everyone started to laugh
"What's wrong with me?" she asked
"I don't know, let's go."
So we jumped in the rocket and flew off to space
I stayed in the rocket
That was ace.

Fia Ord (9)

Portsoy Primary School, Portsoy

My New Friend

Snuggles lives on a rainbow
Snuggles is cute and fluffy
She is three in alien years
She makes rainbows near funfairs.
One day, I was at the funfair
I saw her, all lonely and scared.
So I ran over and gave her a hug
And she followed me all the way home.
My parents let me keep her
We had so much fun
Every day was a blast
Snuggles was my new best friend!

Teagan Rose McLeod (9)
Portsoy Primary School, Portsoy

Slimy Prince

I'd like to be a slimy prince
It would be a dream come true
I'd have a scary castle
With a curvy carriage too
I'd invite slimy, soggy, wet friends too
We'd eat jelly ice cream
For breakfast, lunch and tea
I'd meet a weird-looking monster
And there'd be lots of laughter
We'd have a royal wedding
And live happily ever after.

Eden McGrath (9)
Portsoy Primary School, Portsoy

Floss

My monster, Floss, is very fluffy
She lives in a world of candyfloss
She hopped on a spaceship one day
Which crashed onto the Earth
She landed in a freaky forest
Then got attacked by a boar
Oh no, she was only four!
Then by a snake and a bear
She had to run for her life
But the spaceship sucked her back up
Sending her back to Candyfloss Planet.

Shannon Leigh Mutch (9)
Portsoy Primary School, Portsoy

My Cuddly Friend

Cutie Pie, the colourful monster.
Lived in the sun.
She had very fluffy skin.
As fluffy as a newborn kitten.
One day, she fell out of the sun.
I was outside that day.
And she fell in my arms.
She was so adorable.
I took her to my house.
From then on, she was my new best friend.
All day and all night long.

Lyla Rose Booth (8)
Portsoy Primary School, Portsoy

Farmer KA Clay

One sunny day in the middle of May
Lived a monster called KA Clay
Today, he had to go away
Bump, bump, bump go the wheels on the truck
"Run! Run! Run!" shouts the sheep from the truck
Thump, thump, thump go the cows from the truck
Today, all the animals ran away
Poor old farmer KA Clay.

Olly McKenzie (8)
Portsoy Primary School, Portsoy

Marcus The Funny Monster

Marcus, Marcus went to Paris
And he visited his new school
But when he got in the class
Everybody laughed and laughed
So all day long, they laughed and laughed
But the next day, it was better
Marcus told some funny jokes
Then everybody laughed and laughed
Because he was the funniest in the class.

Bella Mathieson (8)
Portsoy Primary School, Portsoy

Ghostie

Ghostie the invisible monster
Was sad because nobody liked him
He lived in Tokyo in a house
His bedroom was dark black
He went to school and got bullied
Some people said, "Are you okay?"
He said, "No! I get bullied a lot!"
One said, "I'll be your friend."

Cameron Eddy (10)
Portsoy Primary School, Portsoy

Run In The Park

My monster, Turbo, is really active
He went for a run in the park
He started to run.

He ran really fast
Then the wind started to blow
He ran even faster
And he fell over
"Ouch!" said Turbo
On his last breath.

Sadly, this led to his death.

R-Jay Robertson (9)
Portsoy Primary School, Portsoy

Carnage

Carnage the Monster is invisible and scary
He has a long tongue in his mouth
Carnage is from a meteor
Carnage lives in Africa
Carnage has no friends
Carnage is a bad monster
Carnage went to Germany to destroy buildings
But was defeated by the Germans.

Kyle Reise (9)
Portsoy Primary School, Portsoy

The Lonely Monster

One cloudy day at a dump.
A lonely monster sat in trash.
The monster was called Jeff.
Jeff was sad but it was Christmas Eve.
Jeff woke up and found a jet.
Jeff was happy and flew to an island.
Jeff found two friends.
They went bowling.

Riley Ethan McLeod (9)

Portsoy Primary School, Portsoy

Glittery Pie

Hi, my name is Glittery Pie
I come from outer space
I am short and have four eyes
I have a spotty face
I went on a walk one day
And then I had a sneeze
Glitter landed everywhere
I ran away and went back to outer space.

Lexi Thomson (9)
Portsoy Primary School, Portsoy

The Lonely One

I met a monster, lonely and sad
I tried and tried to make him laugh
I tried and tried to make him glad
But he still looked sad
So I took him to the shop
To get him a Fab
Hopefully he was glad...

Laura Sophie McManus (8)

Portsoy Primary School, Portsoy

Jimmy Rages!

Jimmy the Monster played a game
Jimmy the Monster thought it was lame
He looked at the toaster and threw it away
No more toast for Jimmy today
Jimmy the Monster went to lay on the sofa for the
day.

Cian Spratt (8)
Portsoy Primary School, Portsoy

Cuddles

My monster woke up feeling happy
My monster, Cuddles, went to play
She fell off the swing and broke her leg
My monster, Cuddles, went to bed.

Mason Taylor (9)
Portsoy Primary School, Portsoy

Florida Fiend

Every time I turn my back, she's there
A bright pink ball of candyfloss
Four bright eyes staring at me
She is quick as lightning
Bouncing down the Florida beach
Desperate for me to play with her
The Florida Fiend, she is as happy as a lark
I want to be friends with this jolly monster
I took her out, on the jet ski
And she was as wet as a fish
So we lay on the white sand to dry
Her pink fur was as soft as cotton balls
She seemed like a thrill seeker
So I took her to Hollywood Tower Hotel
And she was as frightened as a sheep
She gave me her phone number to stay in touch
More of a friend than a fiend!

Kerys McGuigan (9)
St Aloysius Primary School, Chapelhall

Wibbley Wibster

Over the hill, not too far away
Wibbley Wibster is coming out to play
He is really excited for his birthday today
The children all yell, "Happy birthday, Wibbley!"
They have a celebration and say, "Hip hip hooray!"
He wiggles a little dance with his big gold eye
"I had an amazing birthday," he claims
"I hope I have as much fun next time I come out to play!"
The monster with the purple jelly really enjoyed today.

Ava Grace Caullay (10)
St Aloysius Primary School, Chapelhall

Here Comes Blobbay

Round the corner, down the way
Lives a monster called Blobbay
He is a big purple blob that's always so sad
But if you get to know him, he might not be that bad
He looks very grumpy and jumps around
I don't know how he does it as he is 800 pounds
He has three large green eyes and a toothless grin
His home is a smelly, dirty, huge bin
He eats all the rubbish inside his home
He is a strange blob who likes to live alone.

Ciara Smith (9)
St Aloysius Primary School, Chapelhall

Stinky Monster

I saw Stinky Monster last night
I dreamt about it, it gave me a fright
It had long, curly fangs for teeth
And its feet smelled like roast beef.

Holly Panton (9)
St Aloysius Primary School, Chapelhall

The Friendly Monster

Once there was a monster
As friendly as can be
Then one day he came and said this to me:

"Will you be my friend?
Pretty, pretty please
I'm all alone every day
No one to say
'Hey,
How are you today?'
So will you come and stay with me?
We can have lots of tea."

Pagan Luna Rose Bernard (10)
St Serf's Primary School, Tullibody

Shape-Shifting-Sheila

Sheila is small.
Her husband is Eric.
Andrew is her son.
Pennsylvania is where she lives.
Eric is small too.
Sheila is bossy.
Her dog is called Hugo.
If her dog bites her, she has her,
For her dinner.
Tina helps Sheila on her missions.
If she fails, she loses her job.
Nina is her boss.
Gilbert is her secretary.
Sheila's mission is in Holland.
Her mission is to catch a robber.
Eilidh is her robber.
In a dark alley, Sheila finds the robber.
"Let me go," says Eilidh.
But Sheila doesn't.
She has completed her mission,
And Sheila's family and job are both safe.

Dylan Williams (10)

The Community School Of Auchterarder, Auchterarder

Senior Petit

Senior Petit had all you can eat
Where he took up all the seats
He ate strawberry creams
Under the oak tree
He'd shake the land
And all the monsters around
All the monsters gathered to see
The making of the eating decree
Where had all the strawberry creams
Chocolate trees and jam buns gone?
Senior Petit! That's all he'd eat
He couldn't move
Even around a room
They had to make him pop
Just to put a stop
They stabbed him lightly on the back
And he deflated in a flash
And all this happened in my right pocket.

Kate Tomczyk (10)
The Community School Of Auchterarder, Auchterarder

Lily's Loveheart

There is a blood-red love heart
On a lovable monster's forehead
Her name is Lily Loveheart
She has two multicoloured eyes, a fluffy body
Also, you won't believe her best friend
Is a fiery, fierce person - sorry, monster.
Lily loves her birthmark
She knows that's what her life
Is supposed to mean
That is why she is loveable
And cuddly and Lily Loveheart
Is the kindest monster ever.

Brooke Lily Nassif (11)
The Community School Of Auchterarder, Auchterarder

Grubby Gru

G enuine apple lover he was
R eady, waiting at his apple tree
U nder his tree, he bumped his head
B ruises erupted, "Ouch!" he said
B *oom* went his toy car as it smashed up
"Y eah!" he said as he grabbed another car.

G rumpy dad grabbed the car
"R eady for school?"
"U h... school?"

Guy Morton (11)
The Community School Of Auchterarder, Auchterarder

Arty Molly

A rt is fun
R ed paint
T ime to paint
Y ellow sun!

M ore time to paint
O range paint
L oves to be creative
L oves to be gentle
Y ellow sand on a beach!

Holly Husband (10)
The Community School Of Auchterarder, Auchterarder

The Cutest Of The Cute

Every year, Curlyfluff enters a competition,
A cute competition where the rules are very simple,
The cutest monster will win 100,000 monster money,
Curlyfluff is very cute, but he can never win,
Although his skin is very fluffy, he has a really long chin,
This year was special, he could also win a lifetime worth of whatever he wanted!
He had to win and he had an idea,
What he would do was very simple,
All he had to do was draw on all the monsters' faces a very large pimple,
But it had to be done late at night.
The next day Curlyfluff got a letter,
Saying he had won without a doubt,
He thought to himself,
That was very clever what I did,
The letter also asked him what he wanted a lifetime supply of,
He chose pasta!

Logan Falconer (10)
Thorn Primary School, Johnstone

Goodie Garry

The monster of green and blue
Just as kind as me and you,
Except he had no friends, none at all
Goodie Garry, oh so tall,
Goodie Garry ran away
Goodie Garry had a bad day.
He went to a shop
The keeper shouted, "Stop!"
Goodie Garry ran away
Goodie Garry was having a bad day.
He came to a pool
Everyone was so cruel.
Goodie Garry ran away
Goodie Garry was having a bad day.
He went down an alley alone
Everyone else was comfy at home,
Goodie Garry ran away
Goodie Garry was having a bad day.
In the morning, he came to a nursery
Everyone was nice to him.

Goodie Garry decided to stay
Goodie Garry was having a good day.

Elizabeth Jane Ellerker (11)

Thorn Primary School, Johnstone

Pretty Pinky's Fun Day

Her name is Pinky
She isn't minky
Smaller than a yeti
Loves to eat spaghetti.

She is really cute
Really is a beaut
Not very hairy
Way bigger than a fairy.

She's pretty and funny
Cuter than a bunny
Slimy like soap
Won't eat me, I hope!

Her best friend is Billy
He is very silly
He loves sweets
They're his favourite treats.

One day, they went to the shop
Then they started to hop

They bought sweets and spaghetti
Then they saw their friend, Yeti.

Then they had a party
And invited Yeti Marty
It was so much fun
That's their day done.

Rebecca Catherine Henderson (10)

Thorn Primary School, Johnstone

Hairy Mary Got Into Trouble

Hairy Mary is small but scary, but loves to cause some trouble
On Monday, she went to the park and then she started to bark
So she got into trouble
Hairy Mary is yellow but
On Tuesday, she ate some bread and she turned red
So she got into trouble
Hairy Mary has a long tongue but that didn't cause much fun because
On Wednesday, she stuck it out and wiggled it out
So she got into trouble
Hairy Mary can shape-shift but
On Thursday, she missed her shift
So she got into trouble
Hairy Mary loves to have fun but
On Friday, she blew a big bubble but she didn't get into trouble
Hairy Mary never got into trouble again.

Cara Craig (10)
Thorn Primary School, Johnstone

Exploding Plums!

Mrs Jack wants her pay raise
Doubled to buy more sour plums.

Mrs Jack is a mechanical shape-shifter
She has fangs as sharp as a minotaur's horn.

Mrs Jack has a big mouth and onions for eyes
And has talons longer than my hairy legs.

Mrs Jack, you're still wandering about
Mrs Jack, are you gonna go and do something else
with your life?
Anyway, remember, Mrs Jack wants her pay raise
Doubled to buy more sour plums
Yeah, she has a temper tantrum and
Causes a nuclear explosion which will kill
everybody
In three... two... one... *boom!*

Damien Elliott (10)
Thorn Primary School, Johnstone

Hello

Mildred the monster
All furry and big
Had a head full of hair
That was actually a wig.

Detachable horns
On top of her head
That she took off to sleep in
On her big, comfy bed.

A land far away
Where Mildred would stay
Alone every day
And no one would play.

One day when Mildred was trying on a coat
She looked out the window
And saw a big boat.

Off the boat
The people would go
Until a little girl came and said, "Hello."

Mildred was happy, you say
This kind little girl
Had made her day.

Sophie Henderson (10)
Thorn Primary School, Johnstone

Billy And Pink

His name is Billy
He's super silly
His best friend is Pink, she isn't mink
Billy loves sweets, they're his favourite treats.

One day, they went shopping
In the shop, they started to hop
They bought sweets and spaghetti
And then they met a yeti.

After that they went for dinner
When they invited Hairy Barey
When they made a big mistake
Hairy Barey ate all the food.

And then did a huge burp
That made the whole place shake
That was a fun day
They wouldn't like it any other way.

Nola Belle Salmon (10)

Thorn Primary School, Johnstone

Tina The Teddy's Mystery

Tina the Teddy was cute, kind and friendly for a monster.
One day, she popped to the shop and bought some bread, the bread cost £10.

Tina said, "Why is the price so high?"
The market man said, "Help us, we are under mind control."

Tina was shocked, so she found a power station on the high street
There was a very obvious sign that said: *Danger, Robot Station.*

Tina opened the door and there were so many buttons
So she just randomly pressed buttons and all the robots turned back to humans.

Katie Ferns (11)
Thorn Primary School, Johnstone

Rainbow Ripple's Journey

Rainbow Ripple lives on a little rainbow and always
has a fab day
She paints the rainbow with her loomy, boomy
colours
Every day, the rainbow will be somewhere new
Phew... the rainbow is blue and in the North Pole
today
Uh-oh, Rainbow Ripple has slipped off the rainbow
tonight
She has to sleep in an icy igloo
Morning! Time to paint the rainbow
All Rainbow Ripple's colours have frozen to ice
Now she has to help the mice paint the igloo really
nice
"I think I'll stick with the mice,
I'm a frosty rainbow!"

Abbi Gordon (11)
Thorn Primary School, Johnstone

There Is A Monster In The Freezer!

I went to the fridge freezer to get some ice cream,
I went to see if I could get some for my mum,
But instead, there was a monster,
A cute and cuddly one.

It said it was from Planet Freeze,
And it said it liked the Earth's breeze,
So it flew down in its little ship, but it was quite a squeeze.

It said the other monsters bullied it because it was cute,
It said its name was Frosty Fluff,
And that it didn't like the heat.

So it flew back to Planet Freeze,
Even though it was quite a squeeze!

Isla McArthur (10)
Thorn Primary School, Johnstone

Friendly Frank

Friendly Frank was born in a bank
Over the deep blue sea.
He wanted to be tough and rough
But he was in a huff with me.
One day, as he was out, he went in the sea
Then he turned into a merman, how could this be?

He stayed for hours and hours as he had no friends
Then someone came, was it a flea or a bee?
No! It was a person, it was me
He got a friend, one in his whole life
Then more and more until he liked me.

Friendly Frank was born in a bank,
Over the deep blue sea.

Katie Ellis Blair (10)
Thorn Primary School, Johnstone

His Football Is A Monster!

My brother plays football all day long,
Every day, every night, all year long.

He has a red ball that he's had since he was three,
And sometimes he doesn't even stop to eat his tea!

One peculiar thing, you know what happened?

My brother's football grew horns and a tail!
And he didn't even notice that it started to hail.

He kicks his ball over the fence, oops!

Who knows how next door are going
To treat this little mischievous ball? Mwahahaha!

Olivia Giuliana Vanni (10)
Thorn Primary School, Johnstone

My Monster

My monster is big and hairy,
And you could say he's scary.
He has big red hands,
As big as pans.
Everyone calls him Scary Steve,
Which sometimes makes him grieve,
At the top of his head,
Which is also red,
He has one big horn,
And loves to eat corn,
Wherever he goes,
He loves to go on the shows,
But everyone runs away,
Because sometimes he forgets to pay
So is he bad or is he good?
It's your choice, but don't be rude.

Jenny McMillan (10)
Thorn Primary School, Johnstone

A Day In The Life Of Fuzzy Fuzzball

Fuzzy Fuzzball loves to play,
Anywhere, any time, every day
Fuzzy Fuzzball loves to sleep,
Anywhere, any time, every day
Fuzzy Fuzzball loves to eat,
Anywhere, any time, every day
Fuzzy Fuzzball loves to play with his feet,
Anywhere, any time, every day
Fuzzy Fuzzball loves to fly,
Anywhere, any time, every day
Fuzzy Fuzzball loves to throw pies,
Anywhere, any time, every day
Fuzzy Fuzzball went to bed,
Anywhere, any time, every day.

Eva Wright (10)
Thorn Primary School, Johnstone

Silly Sam's Bad Day

Silly Sam, fluffy and friendly,
Silly Sam, funny and crazy,
He is purple and blue,
With his tail wiggling too.

Silly Sam went to the shop,
The shopkeeper wore a funny top,
Silly Sam bought a Crunchie,
It was very yummy.

Then he bought an ice cream,
So he was walking home,
It splatted all over his face,
Silly Sam was having a silly day.

Sam William Tennant (10)
Thorn Primary School, Johnstone

I Met A Friendly Monster

Today I met a monster,
He is funny, kind and sweet,
His favourite animal is a lobster,
He is the cutest monster you'll ever meet.

They call him Ginger the Jokester
He likes to play sports, but trust me, he's not a
cheat,
Here's the weird thing, he doesn't like other
monsters,
Shhhh! Don't tell, but he has very smelly feet.

Caitlin Neil (11)
Thorn Primary School, Johnstone

Mr Big

Mr Big was born on a rig,
He was born with a spade to dig,
He dug and dug just to get off the rig,
He was ready to go, to dig alone.

Then one day, he decided to change his name,
To Mr Dig Who Was Born On A Rig,
For now, he was Mr Dig Who Wished To Dig,
And not Mr Big Who Was Going To Work On A Rig!

Janey MacLellan (10)
Thorn Primary School, Johnstone

Betti The Yeti

Up in the mountains
On a dark, dark day
There was a yeti called Betty
Sitting in her cave.

It wasn't very fun
She felt really dumb
Her mind was running
Like a train.

Her mind started to froth
Then started to bubble
And then her brain popped
And fell into rubble.

James King (11)
Thorn Primary School, Johnstone

The Stinky Monster Takes A Bath

Once there was a very stinky monster called
Harvester
He was very stinky because all he ate were
harvesters
And he never took a bath once.
Then his friend, Bob, tricked him into taking a bath
The plan worked, Harvester fell in the bath
And loved it so much he said he would never leave.

Isaac Green (10)
Thorn Primary School, Johnstone

Silly Sam Jr

Silly Sam Jr loves to play
Silly Sam Jr plays all day.

Silly Sam Jr loves to fish
Silly Sam Jr is fishing all day.

Silly Sam Jr loves food
Silly Sam Jr eats all day.

Silly Sam Jr goes to sleep
Silly Sam Jr sleeps all day.

Ryan Duncan (10)
Thorn Primary School, Johnstone

Silly Suzy

Suzy's really silly
Her besties are Pinky and Billy.

She really likes fire
It's her greatest desire.

She's very short
And she doesn't snort.

She really likes bunnies
But she's not very funny!

Taylor McKay (10)
Thorn Primary School, Johnstone

Frank The Freek

One day, I met Frank the Freek
He had a big beak and loved to eat meat.

He had a moustache
And loved to stash his cash.

He always robbed banks
And loved to pull pranks.

Ryan Craig (10)
Thorn Primary School, Johnstone

YOUNG WRITERS INFORMATION

We hope you have enjoyed reading this book – and that you will continue to in the coming years.

If you're a young writer who enjoys reading and creative writing, or the parent of an enthusiastic poet or story writer, do visit our website **www.youngwriters.co.uk**. Here you will find free competitions, workshops and games, as well as recommended reads, a poetry glossary and our blog.

If you would like to order further copies of this book, or any of our other titles, then please give us a call or visit **www.youngwriters.co.uk**.

Young Writers
Remus House
Coltsfoot Drive
Peterborough
PE2 9BF
(01733) 890066
info@youngwriters.co.uk